The sun will shine again

Lynn Anderson

India | USA | UK

The sun will shine again © 2023 Lynn Anderson

All rights reserved.

No part of this publication may be reproduced, stored in a retrieval system, or transmitted, in any form or by any means, electronic, mechanical, photocopying, recording or otherwise, without the prior written permission of the presenters.

Lynn Anderson asserts the moral right to be identified as the author of this work.

Presentation by *BookLeaf Publishing*

Web: www.bookleafpub.com

E-mail: info@bookleafpub.com

ISBN: 9789358319705

First edition 2023

To Marc, Declan, Brandon, Ethan and Corey and my inspirational Gran Shinny who always reminded me that no matter what the sun would shine again.

ACKNOWLEDGEMENT

I would like to thank all my family and friends who listened to my poems, gave their feedback and encouraged me at every stage. I am grateful for all your support.

PREFACE

The Sun Will Shine Again is a book of hope, examined through a selection of easily relatable poems of the author throughout her late teenage years to date. Poems of love, tears, and growing through adversity.

Alone

No-one understands the way I feel,
The despair inside I cannot reveal
Worthless feeling. I have no cause,
This is no act, I don't want applause.

People around getting uptight
With the sad lonely person who is losing their fight.
No-one to explain the numbness inside
Just close out the world, find somewhere to hide.

It's funny how people surround you all day,
Yet the loneliest girl is stood in their way.

The will inside to fight has vanished.
The life I had has now been banished.
Another tear runs from my eye

Another breath turns to a sigh.

Darkness all around, no light in sight.
Permanent sadness through day and at night.
Annoyance of others makes it clear,
Maybe one day I'll disappear.

Loneliness

Like an earthquake my soul has split
Driving the destruction into my heart
Exploding like a volcano, secreting loneliness
Only concealed in the very depths of my eyes

My head numb with nothingness
My mind ringing with hopeless despair
Ticking away like an unidentified time bomb
Tick..Tick...Tick

My head is a battleground
Negative thought, positive thoughts, battle it out
Like a devil on one shoulder, angel on the other
Who will triumph?

Inspiration, motivation, why have you deserted me?
Abundance of love I have to give, yet so many years without laughter
Life passing so quickly
Positivity is a traitor, filling my head with false hope.

Why am I here? What is life about?
My family are precious but my happiness is lost,
At a crossroads? It needs a map to find me and make me complete.
Loneliness be gone!

Unconditional Love

For two very special people
Who have helped me through thick and thin
For all the times you've held my hand
When my life has been so grim.

You have shone a torch to lead the way
Through my sadness and despair
When I open my heart and cry
I know you will be there.

You shield me from my problems
You dry away my rain
You buy the biggest boxes to pack away my pain.

You wrap me in warm blankets
So gentle and so safe

You sing the sweetest lullabies
To re-ignite my faith.

I love you both very much
I hope you will never forget
If only love was money
I would never be in debt.

Shadows Of Heaven

Far away a memory lies
Over the waters of silent cries,
Where the wind blows gently on your face
And life is edged with a fearless race.

Where golden wishes grow on trees
And kindness brings you to your knees,
A life where meaning has no time
And placid rhythm needs no rhyme.

A loving light leaks from the sun
A brand new day has just begun
Where imagination cannot be doomed
And precious life is not presumed.

Mental War

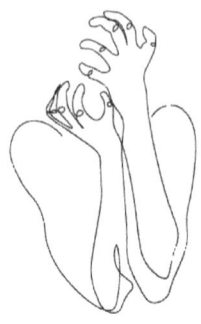

An encaptured heart
In a tormented battle
On an enraged sea
Of unsettled destiny

The unsinkable ship
That refuses to drown
A silent cry
Of pure frustration

Stormy weather
With stubborn rain
Come wash away
This mental war

Heart and Soul

My soul, your heart
We're separated
When we lived apart
Wandering aimlessly
In a lonely dimension
Seeking wrong people
For love and attention

My heart, your soul
Not two halves
But one whole
Never divided or
Drifting astray
Separation again would be
A tragic relay.

You Are...

Every heartbeat that I feel
Every smile I do reveal
Every breath I'm glad to take
Every reason to lie awake

The fiery passion in my eyes
The inspiration in my skies
The pulsating love through my veins
The antiseptic for my pains

Every shiver down my spine
Every reason for me to pine
Every soft sensual whisper spoken
Every shiny penny and lucky token

Every good thought in my head
Every nice word to be said
Every warm glow I feel within
Every bad food that is a sin

The warm soft covers caressing me over
My lucky green four leaf clover
Every taste that is so sweet
Every man I wish to meet.

Sun Through The Clouds

Fall in love with the forbidden moon
and watch the shooting stars of
dynamic destiny come tease you with
her enchanting pulsating passion.

Lend your healing heart and sentimental
soul to the dark sky, to light it up
when the clouds get stormy and he
will forever be in awe with your trusting
compassion.

Forget the world outside, lock in the love
Hold tight and don't let go
Indulge in the love that is truly deserved
and a forgiven freedom will take you into a
timeless trance of happiness.

Now Or Never

Is she the one?
Does she make your life better?
Is she all that you hoped
since the day that you met her?

Does she live up to all
your dreams and desires?
Is her need to be loved
something to admire?

Does she make you believe
that true love is real?
Is she different from others?
Does she help your pain heal?

Does she take away rainclouds
and fill them with sun?
Do you look forward to seeing her
and having fun?

Is she your first thought in the morning
And last thing at night?
Do you ache when she leaves you or is out of sight?

Do you ever look into her eyes
and see her heart breaking?
Do you rescue that hurt
or leave her forsaken?

Could she love you anymore
than what she has felt?
Is the ice in your heat
ready to melt?

Is she looking for answers
for your love for her untold?
Will you ever reveal them
or leave her out in the cold?

Do you think you would miss her
if she was no more?
Or would you tell her
she's the one you adore?

Will time run by?
Will love wait?
Is it time to decide
If she's your soulmate?

Losing Me

Perhaps one day you will
I can only live and learn
Words can speak so easily
Actions cause concern

Hugs that feel so empty
Kisses short not sweet
Living in separate corners
Hearts in different streets

I want to reach out to you
but tears have drowned my heart
My arms are just not long enough
I feel so torn apart

Your eyes say 'what a pity'
Your face filled with regret

Your heart will never love me
I'm just another debt

It only hurts when I think about it
That's only when I breathe
Your face can no longer cover up
The vibes that I conceive

My barriers have risen up
It's fate that does decide
I'll hold on to my love for you
And behind my smile hide

Why?

Why did you do that to me?
What did I do?
Why were you so mean?
Why did I let you?

You enslaved my spirit and threw it around
You snatched out my heart without making a sound
You cut my wrists open, let my insides die
Left me with just enough breath for a sigh

Destroyed all my faith, deprived me of trust
Now the need to heal is a must
Why did you scar me and make me insane?
Why did you leave my mind in such pain?

Now I must analyse each and everything
Never feel like I can win
You made me feel needy, like I was a freak
You took my power and left me weak

Now I must gather all my broken pieces
Hoping one day my fire increases
That I am the camel and this is the straw
My empathic heart now has to withdraw

Courage

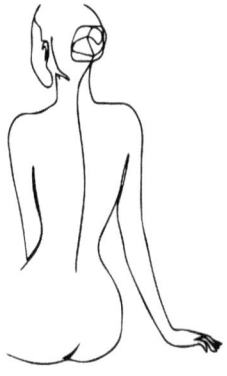

A symbol of courage
when I'm in a lull.
A painted reminder
you've got this girl!

A mark on my skin
to remind me I'm strong.
To stand in my power
when behaviours are wrong.

Tiny Little Miracle

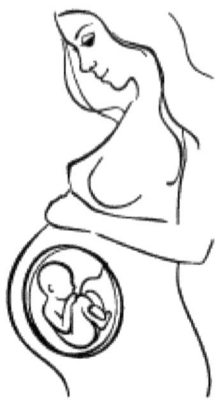

A spark ignites, connection made
The universe conspires, destiny played
A precious miracle against the odds
Two blue lines, excited applause

A tiny heartbeat faster than mine
A rounder body I have to resign
My nutrition and vitamins help you grow
And soon enough you begin to show

The shape of your limbs poking through my skin
Little bubbly ripples makes my heart sing
My hand over my bump, protective and steady
Practising for the rest of your life already

I can't wait to meet you
and hold you so tight
You will be my priority
through day and in night

I carry this precious cargo around each day
Nine months later without delay
For the very first time I see your face
Never have I felt a more powerful embrace

Soul Sisters

So sacred are my soul sisters
Connected by common intent
A bond through shared understanding
Not my blood, more heaven sent

Comfortable in their energy
They keep me vibing high
Understand me on a different level
Make me laugh instead of cry

Accept me fully as I am
Have witnessed worst and best
So safe in their company
No need to second guess

Light my world up like a rainbow
They add texture to my life

Allow my voice to be heard
Without my opinions causing strife

Each reminds me of my song
When I am lost or feeling low
Hold space and let me breathe
Take my hand and allow me to grow

Strong resilience, my female warriors
My kindred spirits for sure
My champions with whom I share a bond
With rebel hearts so pure

Each a different piece of my jigsaw
On this journey we stride each day
I cannot imagine my life without them
They are my compass showing the way

We are all fighting our own battles
Slaying demons day and night
But I am grateful for every one of them
Who support me in my plight

Head space

Just pause
Stop and think
Catch your breath
Take time to sync

Breathe in, breathe out
And just stand still
Why all the rushing?
That stress can kill

Appreciate each moment
Be present in each thought
Practice love and gratitude
Then happiness is sought

Be comfortable in the silence
It lets you hear within
Your inner voice is reasoning
Clearer thoughts begin

Slow down, take in the beauty
Appreciate the grace
A gentle breeze that blows your hair
Or warm sunshine on your face

Children laughing, such innocence
Fresh with all they see
When did we lose our inner child?
So inhibited and care free

Caught up on the treadmill
Running with life's fast pace
Stop trying to meet demands
In surviving life's rat race.

Blue Hearts

My boys are my whole world
Make me so proud that I could cry
I will love them unconditionally
Until the day I die

They will never have to wonder
If I love them or I care
I show them every single day
That no one could compare

As I sit quiet to watch them
They make my heart feel whole
Define my very existence
Paint the canvas of my soul

The magic of dynamics
Life lessons as you grew
Tidal waves of irony

Of who was teaching who

Their ages really differ
As do their wants and needs
Water them with love and affection
To nourish my growing seeds

Their love for me is priceless
No greater gift transcends
I'm blessed and truly grateful
To have grown my five best friends.

Talking to myself

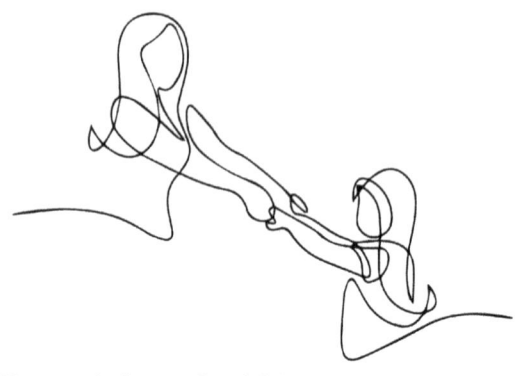

"You remind me of a girl,"
"Which girl?" the girl asked
"A younger version of myself
a memory of the past"

"What was your childhood like?"
"A little sheltered, secure and safe"
"Lynn, it's time for bed now!"
So she turned and gave a wave

I watched as mum tucked her in
Our mother looked so young
She kissed my tiny forehead
And to her neck I clung

Then beyond our mother's gaze
She was settled by my smile

I felt jealous of her safety net
I had not felt for a while

After mum had left her
Of the future she did query
"Will I be happy when I'm older?"
My eyes filled up a little teary

"Our love is taken for granted
but we give it anyway
we are hurt by people's actions
in what they do and say"

"We try to stay connected
to the kindness we were taught
We credit hearts the same as ours
but really they are not"

"We learn so many lessons
like a record on repeat
sometimes we get to move on
other times we find defeat"

"Time passes we get stronger
self-worth begins to dawn
no longer we're walked over
or treated like a pawn"

"Believe in yourself and don't trust fear

as fear is just an illusion
it dashes hopes and tricks your brain
to arrive at the wrong conclusions"

"Remember no matter what, life goes on
hopes and dreams are not for sale
the love you have inside your heart
is what truly will prevail"

"Now settle down now little one
your life is just beginning
enjoy each soothing lullaby
our lovely mum is singing."

Sensitive Survivor

Don't worry gentle soul
I see you
You don't have to try so hard
You are unique in every way

Don't worry gentle soul
I hear you
No need to explain yourself
All words are superfluous

Don't worry gentle soul
I feel you
Your energy transcends my very essence
You are enveloped in my love

Don't worry gentle soul
Just be yourself
Never doubt your worth
You will always be priceless to me

Cinders

Another day in paradise
It's just approaching eight
Rushing around already
She's excessively ornate

Down to get the kids dressed
Don't forget to feed the dog
She puts a load of washing in
Gifts the fire another log

Stacks away the dishes
Drying from the night before
Quickly puts the kettle on
As she mops the kitchen floor

Time for work already
Grabs her bags and makes a dash
Six and a half hours of work
In return for monthly cash

When the working day is over
Her second shift commences
Dance date with the hoover
Over stimulated senses

No fleets of little animals
Coming to lend a hand
She clearly is no Snowwhite
Or the fairest in the land

No handsome Prince is coming
To save her from her chores
The girl is her own warrior
No need to open doors

Dinner made, stock up the fire
She needs to walk the dog
Catch her breath for a moment
Then back to the daily slog

Time to get the boys to bed
Whilst doing a washing spree
She reads another tale
Of untrue reality

Where is her fairy godmother
Or the genie with the wishes?
Back downstairs, prepare tomorrow's lunch
And washes up more dishes

Her day is never ending
Sometimes she's close to tears
Where is evil maleficent
She could sleep one hundred years

Mirror mirror on the wall
This daily toil does hinder
The fires out, her will is weak
All that remains is cinders

Hope

Whenever I lose my sunshine
Or my rain comes pouring through
When I feel I've lost all faith in life
I know I still have you

You give me hope beyond belief
I thought I would not find
Your gentle reassurance
Frees my eyes from being blind

I'm going on a journey
I don't know where I'll land
But I know I'm going to make it
With you to hold my hand

I know when I feel lonely
Or when I'm feeling blue

That's when you're not beside me
I know I'm missing you

The Sun Will Shine Again

Dark days never last too long
Soon the clouds release their rain
And everyday there comes new hope
That the sun will shine again

Milton Keynes UK
Ingram Content Group UK Ltd.
UKHW020938220424
441551UK00019B/1430

9 789358 319705